AMAZING MOUTHS AND MENUS

by Mary Blocksma

illustrated by Lee J. Ames

Prentice-Hall, Inc.

Englewood Cliffs, New Jersey

Book design by Constance Ftera

Printed in the United States of America   ·J

Prentice-Hall International (UK) Limited, London
Prentice-Hall of Australia, Pty. Ltd., Sydney
Prentice-Hall Canada, Inc., Toronto
Prentice-Hall Hispanoamericana, S.A., Mexico
Prentice-Hall of India Private Ltd., New Delhi
Prentice-Hall of Japan, Inc., Tokyo
Prentice-Hall of Southeast Asia Pte. Ltd., Singapore
Whitehall Books Limited, Wellington, New Zealand
Editora Prentice-Hall do Brasil LTDA., Rio de Janeiro

10   9   8   7   6   5   4   3   2   1

Library of Congress Cataloging in Publication Data

Blocksma, Mary.
   Amazing mouths and menus.

   Summary: A varied menu and list of animal guests
for each day of the week demonstrate the kinds of
food different animals eat and how their mouths are
adapted to their individual eating habits.
   1. Animals–Food–Juvenile literature. 2. Mouth–
Juvenile literature. [1. Animals–Food habits.
2. Mouth] I. Ames, Lee J., ill. II. Title.
QL756.5.B56 1986   596′.053   85-9361
ISBN 0-13-023854-6

CONTENTS

ALL KINDS OF MOUTHS

It's amazing how many different kinds of mouths belong to the animals on our earth. Although most of those mouths do have a tongue and a pair of jaws, there is little else that they all have in common. Most animals are picky eaters, and each kind of animal needs just the right kind of mouth to help it eat what it likes best. The more particular an animal is about what it eats, the more special—and often strange—is its mouth.

You would think that the animals in a group—mammals, for example, or birds, fish, or reptiles—would eat much the same food as the other animals in their group. They don't, though. Still, the members of each group sometimes do share certain mouth features or eating habits.

Basic Mammal Mouths

Cats, wolves, bears, whales, deer, and mice are some well-known mammals. Although mammals don't agree on what is good to eat, most of them have a tongue, a pair of jaws, and two rows of teeth that grow out of their jaws. The first teeth, or baby teeth, often fall out. They are replaced by new teeth. If these second teeth are lost, they are usually gone forever. No new teeth grow back. Does that sound familiar? It should. You are a mammal, too.

Most mammals, including you, have three kinds of teeth. The front teeth—the ones you lost first when you were young—are called *incisors*. These are used to cut food. Mammals have four incisors on top and four on the bottom.

Next to the front teeth, sticking out like guard teeth, are the *canines,* sometimes called "fangs" when they are big enough to look dangerous. The canines are handy for tearing food into mouth-sized chunks or for getting a good grip on dinner.

The back teeth, called *molars* or jaw teeth, are used for chewing. Big, flat, and strong, molars grind up pieces of food that are too big to swallow.

The size of each kind of tooth depends not only on the size of the animal, but also on what and how it eats.

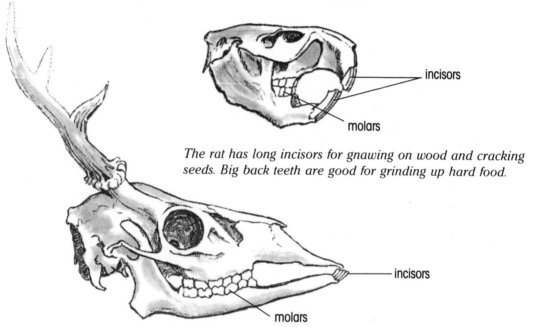

incisors

molars

The rat has long incisors for gnawing on wood and cracking seeds. Big back teeth are good for grinding up hard food.

incisors

molars

The deer eats leaves and plants. It has no front teeth on top and only small ones on the bottom. It needs big molars for grinding up big mouthfuls of leaves.

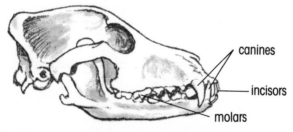

canines

incisors

molars

The wolf eats meat. It has big canines to help kill its supper and then tear it into smaller pieces for swallowing.

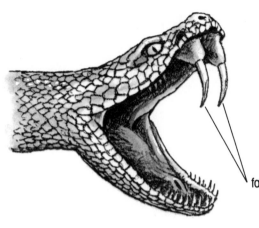

The rattlesnake has big fangs for killing its prey. The fangs are hollow, so poison can shoot down through them. The fangs also help the snake push its dinner down its long throat.

fangs

Basic Reptile Mouths

Most people find it hard to hug a snake or love a lizard. Maybe this is because reptiles have, from people's point of view, terrible table manners. For one thing, having no molars, most reptiles don't bother to chew their food. Some catch supper on the wing with long, sticky tongues. Others stuff down dinner in one lengthy bite, using sharp, curved fangs. Most reptiles swallow dinner whole, in one huge gulp. All in all, reptiles have a rather repulsive way of eating.

Like other animals, each kind of reptile has its own favorite foods. And each has a special, custom-built mouth to help get the good stuff down.

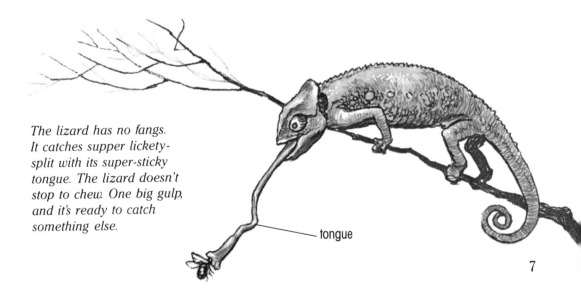

The lizard has no fangs. It catches supper lickety-split with its super-sticky tongue. The lizard doesn't stop to chew. One big gulp, and it's ready to catch something else.

tongue

7

The stickleback fish eats young mosquitoes that float on top of the water. So this fish's mouth points upward.

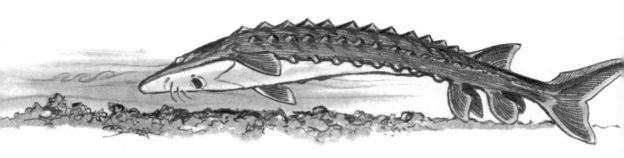

The skate is a bottom feeder. Its mouth is underneath.

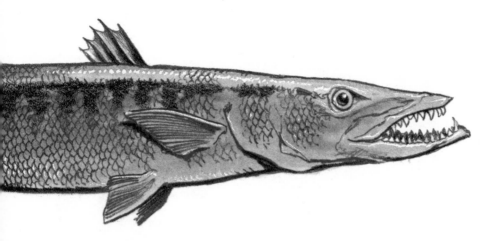

Guess what the barracuda likes to eat?

Basic Fish Mouths

Almost all fish have teeth. But unlike mammals, few of them have chewing teeth. Instead, fish usually sink rows of pointed, pin-sharp teeth into their food to keep their slippery dinners from swimming away. Most fish, like reptiles, swallow their food whole or in good-sized chunks.

In most animals, the mouth is right at the front of the face. Not so with a fish. Its mouth may be under its head so it can scrape food from the bottom, or on the top of its head so it can catch supper in flight. Long, pointed mouths with big jaws full of needle-like teeth belong to fish that eat other fish.

Oddly, fish teeth are not stuck firmly in the jaw the way yours are, so a fish's teeth fall out easily. This does not bother the fish at all. The lost teeth are replaced in only a few weeks as new ones grow back in. Some fish even have teeth growing on their tongues.

Like the animals in other groups, all fish do not like the same things for dinner. Some kinds of fish feed on other fish. Others enjoy insects and worms. Still others eat weeds. Some big fish, like sharks, sometimes swallow a big, swimming mammal.

Basic Bird Mouths

Millions of years ago, some birds may have had quite a fierce set of teeth. Today, however, birds have no teeth at all. Instead, they have either a hard pointed beak or a shapely bill. Even the proud eagle is toothless.

A beak or bill works just as well as teeth, though. And the kind of mouth a bird boasts depends, again, on what a bird eats. Birds are as fussy about food as most other animals are. Some kinds of birds like seeds. They need beaks strong enough to crack open hard shells. Other kinds of birds like insects. Some of them have beaks that can dig bugs out of wood. Still other kinds of birds like meat. Meat must be torn into pieces small enough to swallow, since birds have no molars to chew with.

Bird beaks are made of horn and are so strong that you might wonder how birds can carry them. Some birds with big beaks look too top-heavy to fly. But most bird beaks are full of tiny holes and are no heavier to carry than a sponge.

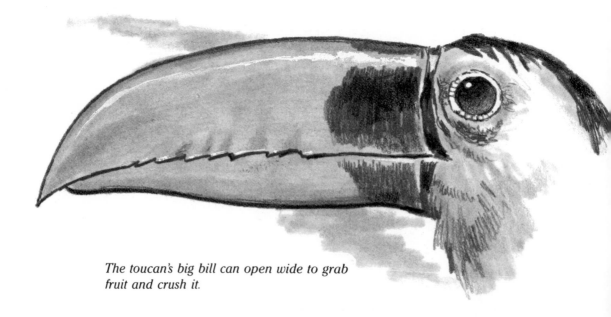

The toucan's big bill can open wide to grab fruit and crush it.

10

The sparrow's little beak is a good seed-cracker.

The meat-eating hawk sinks a powerful, hooked beak into prey so it won't get away.

The woodcock likes bugs and its beak can reach into tiny insects' hiding places.

11

The pelican carries its supper-scooper with it everywhere. It likes to eat fish.

The kind of mouth an animal has depends as much on what it eats as the group of animals it belongs to. To find out how this works, you are invited to a special week of feasts. Each day of the week, the menu will offer a different kind of food. For example, the menu for the first feast will feature some tree parts, a few kinds of rock-hard ocean coral, and some nuts and seeds.

MONDAY'S FEAST

Menu

Tree Parts
Deep Sea Coral
Nuts and Seeds

Today's guests will all be *herbivores.* Herbivores are animals that eat plants. You need a strong beak, big front teeth, or a clever pair of hands to manage today's feast.

Rodents

Among the guests today is the whole rodent family—rats and mice, chipmunks and squirrels, beavers and porcupines. This is one group of animals that knows how to gnaw, and they have the front teeth to prove it. The front teeth of rodents *never stop growing,* so rodents spend most of their lives keeping their teeth ground down to size. To do this, they chew on hard foods with their front teeth, or even grind their front teeth against each other. Rodents also have a good set of molars in the back for grinding food up.

However, they have very short tongues. A rodent can't stick out its tongue the way you can!

Beaver

One of the largest members of the rodent family is the American beaver. The beaver has four huge front teeth, two on top and two on the bottom, that are protected with a hard, orange covering. These super-teeth are so strong that the beaver can scrape bark off trees. It can even gnaw the whole tree down. Sometimes the beaver does this for food. Other times, it uses the trees to build its home or help dam up a stream.

If you chewed down a tree, it would hurt, because unlike the beaver, you have a fine set of nerves in your front teeth. Even worse, you'd get a mouthful of wood chips. The beaver doesn't have that problem, because it has a handy flap of skin behind its front teeth to keep the wood chips out of its mouth. When the beaver does want wood for dinner, its strong back teeth grind it up. These back teeth don't keep growing like the front teeth. But if the beaver didn't keep gnawing, its incisors would grow as long as your hand in just one year.

Parrotfish

Not only is the parrotfish green, much like the parrot that flies, but its mouth also looks much like a parrot's. Its beak and teeth are just right for scraping off bits of hard coral, the favorite dish of this fish.

Cockatiel

The cockatiel's tough, curved beak can crack open the hard seed shells on today's menu. Then its thick, round tongue gets rid of the hard shells fast. The cockatiel has more taste buds on its tongue than most birds do, but it still doesn't have many—only about 100 taste buds. (You have about 9,000 taste buds on your tongue.) Nobody seems to know whether things taste better to animals with a lot of taste buds.

There don't seem to be any reptiles at today's dinner party. They turn up their noses at things hard to chew. (Remember! Reptiles have no molars in back for chewing.) But if you like nuts, you can come. Your front teeth are puny compared to the beaver's, but then, you don't need to crack the shells with your teeth. You have something most animals don't have—hands. You can use tools, too. So let's get cracking and join the gnaw-ful noise!

The cockatiel uses its beak to open one tiny seed at a time.

TUESDAY'S FEAST

Menu

Leaves
Grasses
Fruits and Berries
Vegetables
Seaweed

Not just anyone can eat the stuff on today's menu—only those with a good set of grinding teeth, or those with some other equipment meant for serious chewing. Today's guests, like yesterday's, will be *herbivores*. They eat only plants. And since most herbivores eat a lot and chew for a long time, this feast will go on for hours and hours and hours. Herbivores spend most of their lives chewing.

Hippopotamus

Just look at those jaws! A four-foot-tall kid, much like yourself, could easily stand up inside a hippo's yawn.

Like you, the hippo has all three kinds of teeth—incisors, canines, and molars. But they don't look much like your teeth. Since the hippo must eat mountains of leaves to keep that big body going, it has special teeth to speed things up. (A full-grown hippo may put away 150 pounds of grass in one night—they seem to like eating in the dark. A grown male hippopotamus often weighs 7,000 pounds.)

The hippo's incisors (those big front teeth) and its canines (called tusks when they get that big) help the hippo gather food. The tusks are also effective weapons. So how is a hippo like a squirrel? They both have pockets in their mouths. The squirrel's pockets are used to transport food, but the hippo's have a different use. When the hippo closes its mouth, those tusks fit neatly into pockets in its top jaw.

canines

incisors

Elephant

Those big elephant tusks are really teeth. Like hippos, elephants have huge canines that help them collect leaves and protect them from meat-eating lions and tigers. To keep going, elephants grind up 300 pounds of hay or leaves every day with their big back teeth.

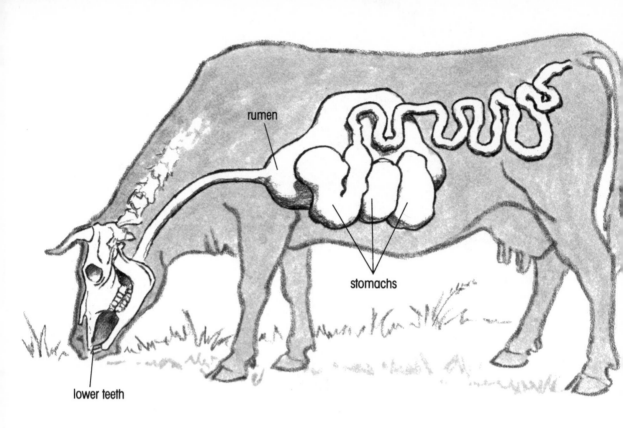

rumen

stomachs

lower teeth

Cow

The cow is missing its two front teeth. Did it get kicked in the mouth? Not at all. Like the deer, the cow has no top incisors. Instead, it has a hard pad on the roof of its mouth. The grass the cow eats goes first to its *rumen,* an organ something like a stomach. There the food is broken into clumps called *cud.* The cud returns to the cow's mouth so the cow can chew it up all over again. After that, the food is swallowed. This time, it goes to the cow's true stomach.

The cow also wins a prize for having a lot of taste buds—14,000 of them on just one tongue! (Remember how many you have on yours?)

Okapi

The deer-like okapi has turned up to show off its long tongue. Its tongue is so long that the okapi can use it like a windshield wiper. It can also wrap its tongue around a branch and strip all the leaves off.

Toucan

Hundreds of birds will come to today's feast, since many birds like fruits and berries. Getting the biggest billing is the toucan. Its big mouth can get around nearly any fruit.

Channel Catfish

The catfish likes plants, especially the ones growing on the bottom of its wet kingdom. The catfish has tube-like jaws full of tiny teeth which scrape plants very well. The mouth sucks up food like a vacuum cleaner.

You are invited to this feast, too. You found plenty to like today. You even like grass. No? Well, corn is a kind of grass. Build yourself a fire and boil up a batch. Or better yet, pop it.

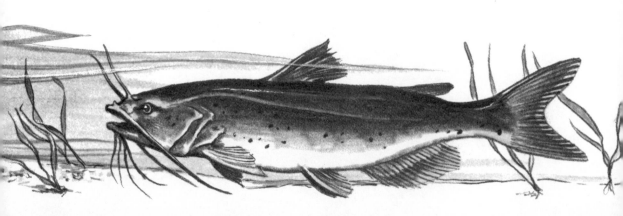

WEDNESDAY'S FEAST

Menu

Raw Eggs in the Shell
Shellfish
Crabs and Mollusks

Animals invited to today's dinner do not have hands and many don't even have legs. So how do they crack the shell of an egg without losing the insides? Or how can they pry open an armored crab to get at the meat? Animals that like their dinners in hard shell packages have developed some neat tricks for dealing with these problems.

Bull Snake

The bull snake takes a great fancy to birds' eggs. It opens its jaws wide and swallows the egg, shell and all. When the egg has gone down its "throat," the clever bull snake thumps its neck on the ground. The egg inside breaks and the snake spits out the shell. The good part runs on down. And down. And down.

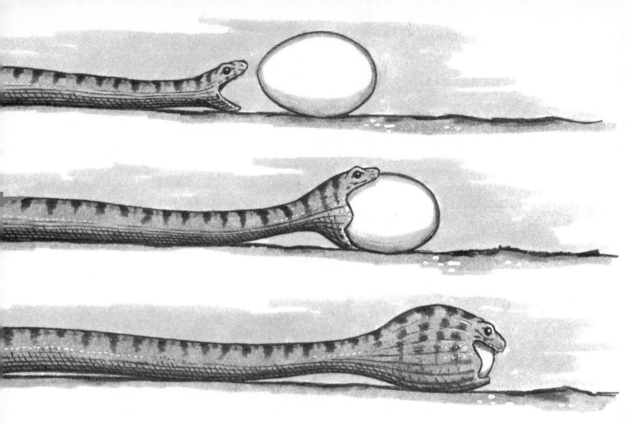

African Egg-Eating Snake

Here is a snake with a different trick for getting into an egg. The African egg-eating snake swallows the egg, but when the egg has gone about an inch down the snake's throat, the snake begins to squeeze. Spikes inside the snake's throat break the egg. The snake just spits out the shell.

Walrus

The walrus has come for clams, and not just a plateful either. A walrus can eat one or two thousand clams at just one sitting.

The big tusks you see are really the walrus's canine teeth. They come in handy for digging clams and other mollusks out of the mud and then prying open the shells. These tusks never stop growing. A good-sized walrus can grow tusks as long as your leg. The tusks are made of ivory and are very heavy. When they are not digging and

prying open food, they make good ice picks to help the big animal move across the hard snow.

The walrus also has huge back teeth which it uses to crush shells. Like the African egg-eating snake, it spits out the shells before swallowing.

Egyptian Vulture

Here's an egg-eating bird for you. The egg-loving Egyptian vulture has a hooked beak so it can pick up an egg. Breaking the egg is easy—the vulture simply drops it on the ground. If the egg is too big

for the vulture to pick up, it picks up a rock instead and drops that on the egg. The vulture doesn't seem to mind eating the yolk off the ground.

Wrasse

Like the walrus, the wrasse likes clams. But this fish has no tusks to help open them. Instead, it has a set of powerful teeth that grow out of its throat. It uses these to crush the shells. Its awful cone-shaped jaw teeth help, too.

You're welcome to come to this feast, because you also have a trick for getting the shells open. You have hands, so you can use tools. You won't need teeth in your throat. Or big tusks, either. How clever of you!

THURSDAY'S FEAST

Menu

Raw Insects

Who'd want to eat an insect? An *insectivore,* of course. You have to be quick to get anything to eat in the crowd that is coming to this feast. A long tongue helps, too. This feast is being held in a damp place buzzing with bugs.

Woodpecker

The woodpecker pays no attention to the flying insects at this feast. Instead, it begins hammering into a tree. The woodpecker finds a tunnel eaten away by insects. Then it snakes its tongue through the tunnel until it catches a bug.

Although the woodpecker's tongue is really quite short, it is attached to a strap too long to fit in the woodpecker's mouth. So where does the woodpecker pocket its tongue? In its nose! It wraps the strap under its jaw, around the back of its head, and hooks the tongue into its left nostril.

Chameleon

The chameleon is a reptile with a different sort of tongue. The chameleon's tongue is about 1½ times the length of its body. If your tongue were 1½ times the length of your body, it would probably be six feet long. Where would you put a tongue that size?

The chameleon has solved the problem of transporting its lengthy taster, for unlike yours, the chameleon's tongue is hollow. When it's not in use, it is kept squeezed onto a bit of pointed bone in the back of the chameleon's throat. There it waits, much like a spring. When the chameleon spots a bug, two sets of muscles send out the tongue like a jack-in-the-box.

Archerfish

The archerfish also has a trick tongue. But its tongue doesn't spring out and it isn't very long, either. Instead, the archerfish curls its tongue against the roof of its mouth to form a tube. Then it shoots drops of water through this tube and tries to hit a bug that sits on a leaf above the water's surface. The archerfish doesn't often miss—the bug falls into the water and the archerfish snaps it up.

Brown Trout

The brown trout has arrived to snap up the bugs on the surface of the water. In addition to small teeth in its jaw, the trout has another set of teeth in the roof of its mouth. It can dine on floating insects. Or it can jump clean out of the water to catch one on the fly.

29

Giant Anteater

Some mammals also like bugs. The giant anteater isn't too quick about getting to its meal. But once there, the anteater shows off a tongue as long as your arm. The amazing tongue is kept in a tube-shaped mouth and is very sticky. It can lick a lot of ants—often 1,000 of them at just one meal.

The anteater can't eat much besides its favorite food. It has no teeth at all, and can only open its mouth wide enough to let in a tongueful of tiny ants.

Your tongue may be a little short for this feast. In some countries, however, people often eat insects. Many insects contain protein, something most often found in milk or meat. Insects can be ground up into a healthful flour, or even covered with chocolate.

FRIDAY'S FEAST

Menu

Blood
Nectar

Today's guests will be on a liquid diet. The only animals expected to show up are those that like to drink dinner instead of eating it. There aren't a whole lot of animals that sip their suppers. But those that do wouldn't have it any other way.

Hummingbirds

Welcome some of the more pleasant supper-sippers, the hummingbirds. If every kind of hummingbird in the world showed up, there would be 320 different kinds.

Sipping nectar from flowers while still in the air is tricky business. But the needle-fine hummingbird bills do a quick and

Hummingbird bills come in many shapes and sizes.

gentle job of it. And it doesn't seem to matter whether the bird has a long bill or a short one, a curved one or a straight one. Once the bill finds the nectar, its hollow tongue sips up the nectar as if through a straw. (Some hummingbirds have sticky tongues, which seem to work just as well.)

Enjoy these lovely creatures. For among the company today are some of the more unpleasant-looking mouths in the world.

Lamprey

The lamprey is rarely welcome to anybody's feast. It sucks blood by biting into the body of a large fish. Before it is through with its meal, the fish will often be dead.

To get hold of its dinner, the lamprey uses a sucking mouth that has no jaws at all. In fact, the lamprey is one of the few jawless animals on earth. Using suction to get a good hold, the lamprey scrapes through the fish's scales with many small, sharp teeth. Once on, the lamprey is hard to shake off. It will stay until it has drunk all the blood it can hold.

This salmon has an unwelcome hanger-on—a lamprey.
The lamprey's mouth works like a suction cup.

Vampire Bat _____

The vampire bat is late for dinner. Because it doesn't like to eat in daylight, it arrives after dark. This is one of the few nights that this bat will drink from a saucer. Like the lamprey, the vampire bat usually feeds on large animals.

Sleeping cattle are frequently victims of the vampire bat. The bat lands on the animal softly—often near the hoof or on some hairless place. Using its sharp incisors (front teeth), the bat first scrapes away a small piece of skin. The bat is so gentle that the animal does not feel anything at all. Once it has made a wound, the bat uses its tongue to sip up the blood.

The vampire bat's tongue is not hollow like a straw. Instead, the bat turns the edges of its tongue down and sets them into a groove in its lower lip. As it draws its tongue back and forth, blood is pulled from the wound into its mouth. The bat may feed this way for a few minutes or as long as half an hour. A bat can drink up to half its own weight in blood. But a bat that gets too greedy often has a hard time flying back home.

Your mouth is not well suited for sipping nectar from flowers. And you probably are not eager to drink blood. So you may want to stay away from this party. It will probably go on past your bedtime, anyway. Vampire bats often don't stop feeding until after midnight.

SATURDAY'S FEAST

Menu

Meat

Today's dinner is for the meat-eating animals, called *carnivores*. This is one tough meal, so each guest will have to have a good set of teeth. Still, most of them won't bother to chew their food.

Most carnivores are also *predators,* or animals that hunt other animals for food. Although carnivores don't eat all day like many herbivores do, it often takes them all day to track down one quick meal. So while most herbivores spend most of their lives eating, most carnivores spend most of *their* lives hunting. It's not easy to catch a supper that is fleeing for its life. So the predator often has a mouth full of sharp teeth which help to make sure that it doesn't go hungry.

Bobcat

The bobcat isn't a very big cat, as wild cats go. But its fangs—or canines—grow nearly as long as the much bigger cougar's. Although the bobcat usually lives on small animals, it sometimes kills an animal a lot larger than itself. Then it uses its fangs to tear off hunks of meat and swallows them without chewing.

The bobcat's tongue is well-built, too. It is strong and almost as rough as a steel woodworking file. The tongue can cut food, help keep food in the bobcat's mouth, and brush the bobcat's coat clean and smooth.

Crocodile

Reptiles like the crocodile also eat meat. But in spite of those awful-looking teeth, the crocodile doesn't use them to eat. Instead, it swallows its food whole, using its great teeth only to catch its dinner. The crocodile seems to be smiling, because its upper canine teeth won't fit in its mouth. When its mouth closes, the big teeth stay outside. They serve as a sharp reminder that the croc has many more teeth inside.

Since the crocodile can't close its mouth all the way, you might think it would choke when it goes underwater. But the croc has special flaps that cover its windpipe and throat and keep the water out.

The croc doesn't worry about losing its teeth. Like fish, crocodiles can easily grow new ones. And since it doesn't chew its food, the croc sometimes swallows a few small stones to help grind up the food that goes down whole. As for the crocodile's tongue, it's stuck. It is rooted to the back of the animal's mouth and will not move.

There are animals in the world that do not fear the crocodile's big mouth. Crocodile babies often ride in there. And the mother crocodile uses her mouth to gently crack the eggs of her young when they are ready to hatch. Then there are the birds that clean the croc's sharp teeth. Several kinds of birds take on this daring job, including the plover, the stork, and the sandpiper. Some even hop inside the crocodile's gaping jaws!

Rattlesnake

Not only does the rattlesnake usually eat its prey in one piece, it hungers after something bigger than its own body. And the rattlesnake can swallow a much larger dinner than anyone would guess by just looking at that mouth. Because its jaws are not hinged tightly, as yours are, the rattlesnake can move them very far apart. It has no chewing teeth, but its fangs help shove the prey down.

The fangs are two hollow teeth that lead to a supply of deadly poison. When the snake bites an animal, the poison is pushed through the tunnels in its fangs. The poison doesn't spoil the snake's dinner, because the rattlesnake is immune to its own venom.

Although the rattlesnake's flickering forked tongue looks dangerous, it's not used for biting. It isn't used for tasting, either, since a snake's tongue has no taste buds. Instead, the rattlesnake's tongue helps the snake smell by bringing tiny bits from the ground and the air to two small pits in the snake's mouth.

Great White Shark

Here's a mouth anyone can respect. The great white shark's mouth is on the underside of its head and is full of very big, very sharp teeth, which the shark uses to tear hunks out of extra-large dinners.

This shark has a row of "working teeth" in front, hard as steel. Behind it are several more rows of teeth. When the front teeth fall out, a whole new row moves forward to replace them. Some sharks get a new set of working teeth every two weeks!

The shark still makes frequent trips to its dentist, a small fish called a remora. The remora cleans the shark's teeth and body so well that sharks often will wait in line for its services.

Whale Shark

The whale shark is the biggest fish in the sea, even bigger than the great white shark. But its mouth is not at all like the mouths of other sharks. The whale shark's mouth is in front of, not underneath, its head. And its mouth is almost as wide as its body.

The great white shark (above) is smaller than the whale shark (below).
But which one would you rather bump into?

Not to worry. This gentle giant's teeth are even smaller than yours are—only ⅛ inch long. And it hardly ever uses them. The whale shark eats only *plankton*, little one-celled plants and animals that live near the surface of the water. Instead of teeth, the whale shark uses *gill rakers*, comb-like strainers that collect the tiny plankton from the water.

Barn Owl

Many birds are carnivores, too. The owl has come to this feast, hoping for a plateful of mouse meat. Since the owl often eats its own weight in rats and mice in one night, many farmers would rather have an owl in the barn than a whole posse of cats! The owl may not have teeth, but not only is its beak very strong, it's also hooked for tearing off bite-sized morsels.

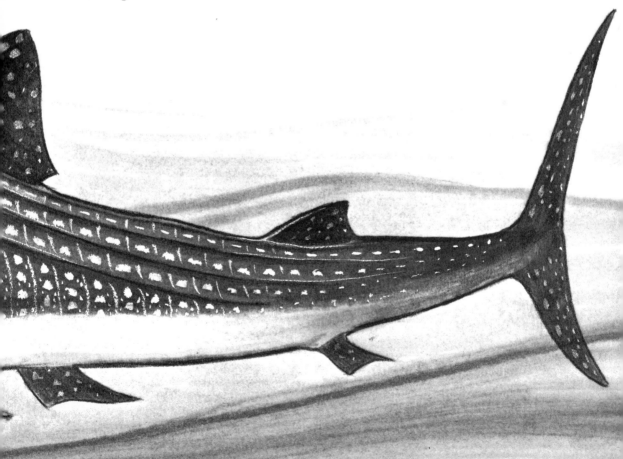

The barn owl is known as a mighty mouser.

Pelican

Birds that eat fish often have big bills for fishing. The pelican, like most fishing birds, has built-in bill-strainers. These strainers keep the bird from swallowing mud with its meal.

Contrary to popular opinion, the pelican does *not* use its bill as a cargo bay. If it tried to fly with a bill-full of fish, the bird would fall on its head. Instead, a pelican that is collecting fish for baby pelicans swallows the fish. Then it flies to the nest and brings the food back up into its bill. The bill does make a good dish for the babies to eat from.

If you don't mind the company, you are welcome to roast a mouse or two. No, thank you? Well, how about a hamburger—to go!

SUNDAY'S FEAST

Menu

Seeds	Honey
Nuts	Milk
Grasses	Juice
Leaves	Eggs
Roots	Shellfish
Fruits	Meat
Berries	Fish
Vegetables	Poultry

Today's feast is not for picky eaters, because today's dinner is for *omnivores,* or animals that will eat practically anything. The animals that come to this feast would probably have found something to enjoy at most of this week's feasts. All they need to do today is eat all the leftovers. Bears, raccoons, pigs, rats, and monkeys will all be here. They're all omnivores. But our most important guest today is YOU!

Human Being

You are the guest of honor, for not only do you eat many kinds of foods, you also like to mix them up. Look what you might do with leftovers from five of this week's feasts:

Seeds give you *wheat* so you can make *noodles.*
Eggs help make *noodles,* too.

Meat gives you *hamburger* so you can make *meatballs.*

Fruit gives you *tomatoes* so you can make *sauce.*
Leaves give you *herbs* so you can season the *sauce.*

Liquids give you *milk* so you can make *cheese.*

Mix all this stuff up, cook it, and you have *spaghetti!* You can do this because you are very smart. No other animal has scored higher on smartness tests than you. Also, you have hands, so you can mix and stir and cook. And of course, you have a set of teeth just made for such a meal.

Like other mammals, you have three kinds of teeth. Because you aren't especially good at swallowing your food whole, you have a good set of molars—back chewing teeth. You also have fangs—the canines—but they are not very big. Bobcats need big fangs for

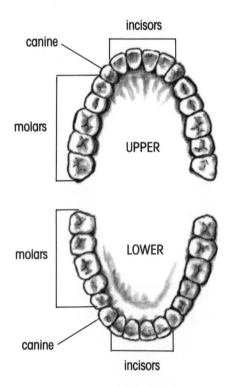

killing, but you don't have to hunt dinner with your mouth. And you can use a knife to cut your meat into small pieces. Your canines do help you tear off bites of sandwich, though. And your front teeth—the incisors—let you snip off noodles too long to fit in your mouth.

Your tongue is ideal for enjoying spicy sauces. It can taste sour things on the sides, salty things in the middle, sweet things at the tip, and bitter things in the back.

THE HUMAN TONGUE

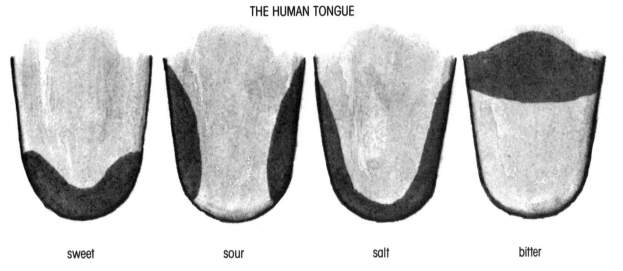

| sweet | sour | salt | bitter |

You also have 9,000 tiny taste buds on your tongue. And because you aren't grown up yet, you have extra taste buds on the insides of your cheeks. (Only children have these, which may be partly why children seem to have such a sharp sense of taste.) And did you know that if you could make a tongue-print, it would be different from anyone else's? The patterns your tongue makes are as unique as the ones made by your fingers.

Louisiana Land Turtle

Though the Louisiana land turtle is totally toothless, it can eat nearly anything you can. The turtle has a beak, much like a bird's. To chew, it crushes food against a hard plate on the roof of its mouth. The turtle likes almost any kind of food—even insects. Its body may not move very fast, but its mouth can snap up a grasshopper on the fly.

Grizzly Bear

The towering grizzly bear is the world's biggest meat-eating land animal—up to nine feet tall and more than 1000 pounds. Keeping that huge bulk fit and fed is one of the bear's biggest problems. It has a powerful mouth to help, though. The grizzly's strong jaws and 40 huge teeth can crunch through almost anything—bones, nuts, or branches.

The grizzly is an omnivore, but its main course changes with the seasons. In spring, the grizzly eats mostly grasses, roots, moss, and bulbs. In summer, the bear goes fishing—especially if it lives in Alaska where the salmon run. The jaws of a hungry bear can snap up a jumping salmon in mid-leap.

In late summer, the bear switches to berries, which it gobbles leaves, twigs and all. It also eats things like mushrooms, deer and rodents, insects, nuts, honey, and dead animals.

By October, a healthy grizzly is well-fed and fat—a good thing, too, because it may not eat again until April! The grizzly literally sleeps half its life away, hibernating (sleeping through the winter) longer than any other animal. It sometimes goes six months without a meal.

Magpie

Here comes the cleanup crew. The magpie will eat almost anything, even meat from another animal's dinner. Its strong, curved beak gives it a real all-purpose mouth. And the magpie is no coward. It has even been seen stealing from an eagle!

Carp

The carp helps keep the lake cleaned up. It will eat nearly anything and is one of the few fish that chews its food. Using a good set of jaw teeth, the carp thinks nothing of crushing weeds, insects, worms, eggs, and bits of other fishes. But the carp only eats in summer. In winter, it settles into the mud at the bottom of the lake and stays there until spring, often without a single meal. It is one of the few fishes that does this.

Well, all you omnivores did a great job of cleaning up. And since many of you have a "sweet tooth," we'll have some ice cream and berries for dessert. Dessert is just for omnivores, since most animals can't taste sweet things. But unless you have a new row of teeth behind the ones in front, you'd better brush the ones you have after this meal. An amazing mouth like yours is worth taking care of.